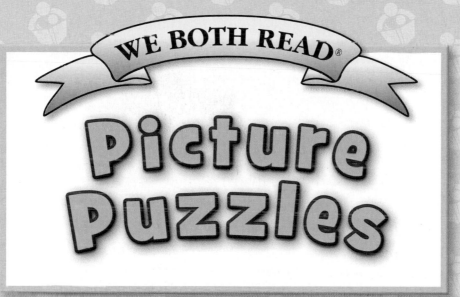

WE BOTH READ®
Picture Puzzles

By Sindy McKay

Picture Puzzles
Parent's Introduction

We Both Read books have been developed by reading specialists to invite parents and children to interact as they read together. This particular book is designed for a parent or adult to read the entire book to a child. However, throughout the book the child is invited to actively participate by looking at the pictures and responding to questions.

In this book, you read the question on the right-hand page. (You may want to run your finger under the words as you read the question.) Then, before turning the page, your child tries to guess the answer. When you turn the page, the left-hand page shows the answer.

Consider encouraging children to think of this as a game or puzzle, which they can solve by looking at and thinking about the pictures. If needed, you can provide support by helping to identify what is in the pictures and asking what is the same or different about them. In some cases you may be able to eliminate some pictures as you discuss what might be the correct answer.

You can give hints to the answer by asking additional questions. For example, if a question is, *Which of these animals is the smallest?*, you could help to identify the animals and then point to two animals and ask which one is smaller. If the question is, *Which animal would you not find on a farm?*, you could help to

identify the animals and ask if it is likely that this animal would be on a farm. You could even expand the discussion to talk about different kinds of farm animals.

Reading this book together will assist in the development of cognitive thinking and learning skills that will help your child in school. Depending upon your child, it may be helpful to read only a part of the book at a time. It may also be helpful to read this book more than once with your child. Most of all, remember to praise your child's efforts and keep the interaction fun.

Try to keep these tips in mind, but don't worry about doing everything right. Simply sharing the book together will help prepare your child for reading, mathematics, and doing well in school.

Picture Puzzles

A We Both Read® Book: Level PK–K
Guided Reading: Level AA

———————————————————

Text Copyright © 2022 by Sindy McKay
Use of photographs provided by iStock and Dreamstime.

We Both Read® is a trademark of Treasure Bay, Inc.

Published by
Treasure Bay, Inc.
PO Box 519
Roseville, CA 95661 USA

Library of Congress Control Number: 2021943697

Printed in China

ISBN: 978-1-60115-367-8

Visit us online at:
WeBothRead.com

PR-10-21

Which animal does not belong on a farm?

The lion.

A lion is much more at home on the plains of Africa than on a farm. Lions hunt during the night and spend most of their days resting.

Which child is eating fruit?

This child is eating an apple, which is a type of fruit.

What kinds of food are the other children eating?

Hot dog

Cereal

Carrot

Which one can run the fastest?

The horse.

There was one horse that was able to run fifty-five miles per hour. That's as fast as some cars go on the highway. That's a lot faster than turtles, snails, or humans can run!

Which building is the tallest?

The skyscraper.

The tallest skyscraper in the world is more than a half-mile high.

Which one is not like the others?

The flower.

The other pictures are all of animals. Can you think of what is different between a flower or a plant and animals?

Lemur   Chameleon

Dog

Which one has the smallest feet?

The mouse.

Did you know that elephants can "hear" with their feet? Their feet can feel the low rumbles of other elephants up to twenty miles away!

Which one does **not** belong
at a picnic?

13

The couch.

Picnics are fun! But why are there always so many ants at a picnic? First, a few ants may visit your picnic to enjoy the food. When those ants return to the nest, they leave a scent trail for all their ant friends to follow back to your picnic!

Which animal would make a good house pet?

The hamster.

Hamsters make great pets! Unfortunately, lots of interesting animals, like gorillas, penguins, and octopuses, wouldn't be good as pets. Can you think of any reasons why?

Gorilla   Penguin   Octopus

Which item might you use on a rainy day?

The umbrella.

You might want an umbella on a rainy day.

When do you think you might use these other things?

Which one is a different kind of animal?

The lizard.

This green basilisk lizard is a type of reptile. It doesn't fly. The other animals are all birds that fly.

Flamingos can often be seen standing in the water on one leg, but they can also fly very fast for long distances.

Which one is not like the others?

The airplane.

An airplane travels through the air. The sailboat, speed-boat and canoe, all travel on water.

Sailboat   Speedboat   Canoe

Which animal has spots?

The cheetah.

The zebra has stripes. Did you know that no two zebras have stripes that look exactly the same?

Which two items would you find on a soccer field?

The soccer ball and net.

You don't usually see a sack of potatoes or a pair of monkeys at a soccer game.

Which picture is showing a different season than the others?

The children jumping in the water.

These kids are having fun in the summer season! The pictures with snow were taken in the winter. When snow melts in the spring, it becomes water that flows into rivers and lakes.

Which of these would you probably not see in a park?

The bed.

Beds are usually found in bedrooms. However, if you were in a park you might find a flower bed.

Which vehicle do firefighters use?

The fire truck or fire engine.

After working hard all day, firefighters might enjoy getting ice cream from an ice cream truck! And when they get home they might get mail that was delivered by someone using a mail truck.

Ice cream truck

Mail truck

Which musical instrument is not like the others?

The violin.

The violin is a string instrument. You play it by drawing a bow across the strings. The trombone, trumpet, and tuba are brass instruments. You play them by blowing into them.

Trombone

Trumpet

Tuba

Which vehicle has
the most wheels?

This vehicle has the most wheels.

How many wheels do you think it has? (Remember to count the wheels you cannot see on the other side!)

Three wheels

Four wheels

Which tool would you **not** use to build a house?

The hair dryer.

A hair dryer might be helpful after the workers take a shower, but it won't help them build the house!

These items are much more helpful!

Saw

Drill

Hammer

Which one is not like the others?

The car.

The car has four wheels. The bicycles have two wheels.

Remember to wear your helmet!

Which animal is the shortest?

The dog.

The smallest dog on record was a Chihuahua (chee-WOW-wah) named Milly, who was only four inches tall. That's shorter than a can of soda! The tallest giraffe was about nineteen feet tall. That's as tall as a two-story house!

Alpaca

Giraffe

Pony

If you liked *Picture Puzzles*, here are some other
We Both Read® books you are sure to enjoy!

To see all the We Both Read books that are available,
just go online to **WeBothRead.com**.